The Tale of the 13 Keys of Love-Together

Written by Michael Takyi

Illustrations by Ebony Backes

The Tale of the 13 Keys of Love-Together

Written by Michael Takyi
Illustrations by Ebony Backes

Once upon a time
in a village not so far,
lived two loving hearts
named Nula and Tars.

Under the moonlight
they danced to the sea,
and thought that their love
would thrive unconditionally.

One day a wise owl, named Gowl

with feathers of gold,

Swooped down and said,

"Here's a tale to be told."

Perched on a branch,

with eyes deep and keen,

a guardian of wisdom,

a keeper unseen.

His voice carried truth,

a melody so grand,

"I've watched over hearts

and the castles they've planned."

"Your love is a castle

with towers so tall,

but to keep it standing,

you need keys

– one and all.

These keys hold the secrets

to love's sturdy walls,

without them,

the mightiest castles will fall."

"Thirteen golden keys,
so shiny and bright,
will guide you together
during good days
and days you fight.
But beware,
sweet love birds,
for if seven go astray,
your castle of love
might crumble away."

Gowl continued to say,
his gold feathers on display,
"I've seen love falter,
I've seen it decay.
But I've also seen couples
rise from despair,
their bonds growing stronger
when they repair."

Nula and Tars inspired,
their hearts filled with cheer,
"We'll find these thirteen keys,
there's nothing to fear!"
So off they went,
hand in hand with glee,
to discover the keys that
would make them happy.

Key One: Mutual Respect

Oh so grand,

to honor each other's

ideas and plans.

"You're so unique," Nula said,

"like a shooting star,

I love how you think,

you're perfect as you are."

As they shared their thoughts

by a bubbling stream,

they built a vision,

a collaborative dream.

Key 2: Shared Vision

A goal they believe in,
dreaming together,
so both could win.
"We'll travel the world,"
Tars said with delight,
"We'll climb mountains,
and reach every height."

Key 4: Adaptability

When things didn't go right,
they learned how to bend
and not hold onto spite.
When plans changed suddenly,
they'd laugh and they'd say,
"We'll make it work,
come what may!"
Together they rebuilt
what had fallen apart,
with laughter and courage,
they restarted their art.

Key 5: Conflict Resolution

"I'm sorry" was stated
after an argument flared.
They'd take a deep breath
and calmly declare,
"I care about you,
let's make this fair."
Under the shade
of a towering tree,
they found harmony,
as love set them free.

"Even if you're afraid,
or ashamed
you can rely on me."
Tars proclaimed,
"I won't judge you,

Key 6: Trust

you can trust me,
I've got your back
whenever you need."
"Catch me," said Nula,
leaping with glee.
Tars' hands steady,
her safety a decree.

Key 7: Emotional Intelligence

Sharing their feelings,

not trying to fix things.

When Nula felt blue,

Tars held her tight,

Saying, "I'm with you,

it'll be alright."

In moments of joy

or moments of sadness,

they'd lift each other

in complete gladness.

Key 8: Physical & Emotional Intimacy

"Lots of hugs & kisses,

to grow stronger their bond.

Their love was a river

flowing above and beyond.

Their bond created

a passionate love

that could weather any storm,

that they were sure of.

By the water's edge,

their hands interwove,

creating a sanctuary,

their garden of love."

Key 9: Financial Harmony

Making plans with a pen,

"Let's save for our dreams

and stick well to them."

They budgeted together,

never spending a lot,

"No silly spending,

let's cherish what we've got."

Coins clinked,

and their savings grew.

Their future secure,

as their dreams came true."

The cookies they'd baked

or swimming in a lake.

"Remember that time?"

Tars would always say,

And Nula
would smile,

"I'll never
forget that day."

Each moment
they lived,
no matter how small,

Became treasures
of love,
their most
precious of all.

Key 11: Support for Individuality

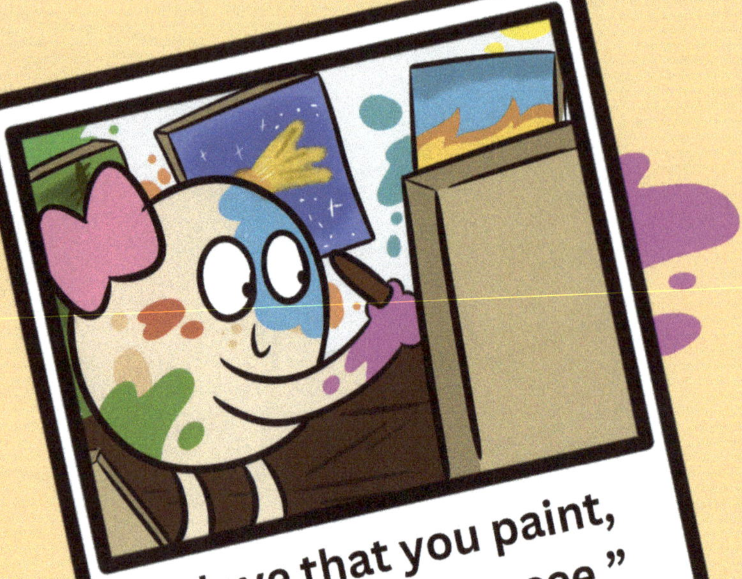

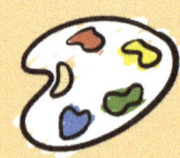

"I love that you paint,
it's so special to see."
Tars respected her talent
and let her be free.

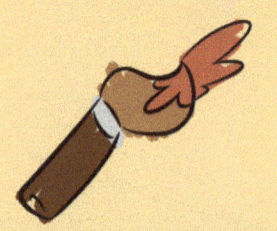

And when Tars
played his guitar
with all of his might,
Nula cheered loudly,
"You're my rockstar tonight!"

Each talent they nurtured,
each passion they fed,
made their love bloom,
vibrant and widespread.

Key 12: Growth

Together they'd strive,
learning new things,
keeping their love alive,
by being better beings.
"We'll keep growing
together,
day by day,
learning and loving,
come what may."
Books they'd read
& dreams they'd design,
their future a tapestry,
woven so fine.

Key 13:
Resilience in Adversity

When life gets tough,

like a hard test,

they'd find a way

to give it their best.

"We'll face it together,"

they'd say with a grin,

"No matter how tough,

our love will win."

Climbing steep hills

or weathering a storm,

their love grew stronger,

its roots kept warm.

Gowl watched closely,
his eyes big and bright,
as Nula and Tars
collected each key in the night.
Through thorny woods
that made it hard to see,
they faced fears
but didn't retreat.

Storms would rise,
and doubts would creep,
yet their love endured,
promises they'd keep.
Each key they found
bore lessons of old,
strengthening their bond,
more precious than gold.

But one day, oh dear,

they stumbled and fell,

burdened by worries

they could not quell.

The weight of the world

pressed hard on their bond,

and doubt whispered fears

they couldn't respond.

Missteps were taken,

trust grew thin,

as external pressures

let discord begin.

They stopped respecting (key 1),
small words turned cold.
Their shared vision dimmed (key 2),
dreams left untold.
Communication faltered (key 3),
silence grew loud,
leaving their hearts distant,
lost in the crowd.

Conflict erupted (key 5),
anger took the stage,
and trust faded (key 6),
replaced by quiet rage.
Emotions ran wild (key 7),
tears flowed like streams,
while harmony swayed (key 9),
shattering their dreams.

The castle of love

broke down from above,

as cracks spread wide,

reflecting the fear & doubt

they could no longer hide.

Each tremor mirrored

the pain they'd concealed.

A reminder of the love

they must rebuild.

Nula cried out,

"Is this a mistake?"

"Let's find those keys,
we must try."

Her voice quivered,
her heart starting
to break.
But Tars took her hand,
with a tear in his eye,
"We'll find those keys,
we must try."

They worked through the night,
till the break of day,
tracing their steps
to where the keys lay.
For respect, they shared words
with hearts open wide.

Apologies mended
what pride had denied.
Their vision returned
as they mapped out their dreams,
setting new goals
under moonlight beams.

With communication,
they spoke truths untold,
breaking the silence that had
left them cold.
Trust was rebuilt

through acts that proved care.
Step by step,
they showed they were there.
Harmony sang as emotions aligned,
restoring the rhythm
where love intertwined.

Gowl fluttered down,

his wings wide with pride,

as the first rays of dawn

lit the countryside.

"Thirteen golden keys –

your love will never die,"

he hooted softly,

under the morning sky.

The castle now gleamed,
a beacon of light.
Standing strong through the day
and glowing at night.

The END

The story
continues on:

www.love-together.com

About Love-Together

Love-Together is a revolutionary platform designed to help individuals and couples discover deeper connections through self-awareness and relationship insights.

Built on key pillars, it offers tools that can help uncover values, align priorities, and strengthen communication.

Whether you're seeking love or growing an existing bond, Love-Together empowers you to understand yourself and your partner better, fostering trust, growth & lasting love.

Go beyond matching—and get the steps to create the foundation for a meaningful and fulfilling relationship.